The Art of Silk Painting

by Christine Mariotti

Many thanks to:
Ryker Photo, for the inspirational photography
Gabriella Lopez, for modeling my scarves in the photographs
Cassie Tondro and Mel Clark, for the opportunity to teach
silk painting workshops at Wildfiber
Susan Louise Moyer, for providing the inspiration for my
teaching and writing

Walter Foster Publishing, Inc.
23062 La Cadena Drive
Laguna Hills, CA 92653
www.walterfoster.com

Contents

Introduction 3

Assembling Your Equipment 4
   Resists and Outliners 5
   Paints and Dyes for Silk 6
   Painting Safely 6

Working with Silk 7
   Types of Silk 7
   Cutting the Silk 8
   Mounting the Silk 8
   Steaming and Washing the Silk 9

Learning to Use Silk Dyes: Making a Color Wheel 10
   Color Wheel Diagram 15

Variegated Pillows: Texturing with Salt 16

Abstract Bandanna: Alcohol Techniques 19
   Bandanna Template 22

Spring Bouquet: Clear Gutta Resist Outlines 23
   Spring Bouquet Template 30

Border View: Landscape with Black Gutta Silhouette 32

Hummingbird and Fuchsias: Gold Resist over Pastel Colors 36
   Hummingbird Templates 39

Classical Koi: Gutta-Outlined Asian Design 40
   Koi Templates 45

Mystery Dragonflies: Gutta Resist over Colored Lines 46
   Dragonfly Templates 51

Tropical Explosion: Wax-Resist Technique 52

Interior Still Life: Painting a Scene 58

Conclusion 64

Introduction

Painting on silk is one of the most exciting avenues of artistic self-expression I know. Silk is a lustrous and supple fabric that reacts beautifully to the brilliant and transparent dyes and paints. An added advantage to painting on silk is that you can just as easily create a wearable garment as you can an accessory or a piece of framed art. And whatever your favorite themes may be—animals, flowers, nature and landscapes, or abstract designs—you'll be able to experiment with them on this versatile surface. Each subject you paint undergoes a magical transformation of texture and color that can be accomplished only by the interaction of dyes and paints on silk.

In Asia, silk paintings were traditionally either displayed as fine screens or worn as kimonos. The inspirational subjects of that culture's past, such as delicate florals and meandering patterns, are still being used by designers today. But now very modern and unusual patterns can be applied with a few simple tools. And with a little practice, even novices will see exciting results in a very short time.

There is little you'll need for success except a love of color and its many variations. But there are also many exciting techniques that will add unusual textures to your paintings. They'll keep you returning to the subject and yearning to express yourself in new and unique ways. So join me on a glorious new creative adventure!

Assembling Your Equipment

Some of the materials you need are specialized for silk painting, but you probably already have many of them in your home or can purchase them at a grocery store or pharmacy. On these pages, I list all the tools and materials you'll need to begin and a few extras that will come in handy as you work. Most silk painting products are available at your local art supply store in the textile arts aisle, but you can also find them through mail-order catalogs advertised in craft magazines or on the Internet.

Tools and Materials Here are examples of the basic supplies I used for the projects in this book, including dyes, gutta, gutta applicators, foam brushes, watercolor brushes, and a washable pencil (available in art supply or fabric stores). I also keep cotton swabs on hand to apply dyes and rubbing alcohol, as well as sea salt for creating special effects. I use an eye dropper for adding small amounts of dye to a mix, and I use a clothespin and cotton ball to blot excess color from the silk.

Basic Supplies

- Silk—lightweight, smooth-surfaced 100% China, or Habotai (see "Types of Silk," page 7)

- Washable pencil—to trace designs onto the silk

- Frames—embroidery hoops or stretcher bars

- Pins—pushpins, architect's three-pronged tacks, or hooks (or small safety pins) attached to rubber bands (see "Mounting the Silk," pages 8–9)

- Dyes or paints—premixed in bottles in a range of colors (see "Paints and Dyes for Silk," page 6)

- Resists—clear and colored water-based or oil-based guttas (see "Resists and Outliners," page 5), beeswax, and paraffin wax

- Plastic gutta applicator with metal tip—to apply gutta resist to the silk

- Paintbrushes—both watercolor and foam brushes (small, medium, and large)

- Plastic cups—in varying sizes, to hold dyes and diluting agents

- Rubbing alcohol—for diluting dyes and creating special effects on dyed surfaces

- Drawing paper—to draw your design before painting

- Masking tape—for small projects, to attach silk to the frame

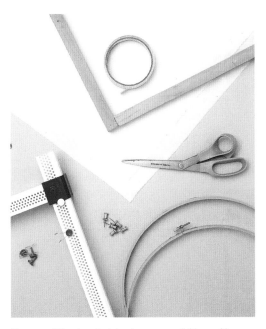

Frames Wooden stretcher bars are available as either stationary frames (a set size) or adjustable frames (see "Mounting the Silk," pages 8–9). You can also buy plastic and wooden frames that come with hooks or pins for attaching the silk. Shown here are round embroidery hoops, wooden stretcher bars, and a plastic adjustable frame.

Extras Plastic bowls and plates make great palettes for mixing colors and templates for drawing circles. A hair dryer will help the dyes and paints dry faster, and a household iron can set gutta and heat-set colors. Use paper towels to clean the tips of gutta applicators and for general cleanup, and wear rubber gloves to protect your hands from stains.

Resists and Outliners

Guttas are thick, syrupy substances that resist the dyes, which is a way of "saving white" or protecting a painted area from other colors: the gutta resists any color applied over it. Water-based guttas are easy to work with because they can be thinned with water. Oil-based guttas must be thinned with gutta thinner or mineral spirits, but I prefer them because they leave crisper lines. When used as a resist, clear gutta is applied before the dyes and then washed out (water-based) or dry-cleaned (oil-based) after the color has set, creating white outlines. When used to create permanent colored outlines, colored gutta must be set; otherwise, it may dissolve when you hand-wash the silk (see page 7). To set gutta, place a layer of tissue paper or fabric over the gutta (to prevent the iron from sticking to the gutta), and press on medium-high for about 1 minute.

Applicators Gutta applicators have small metal screw-on or push-on tips that allow you to apply smooth, fine lines. You may have to secure the tip with a little masking tape to prevent it from slipping off as you squeeze. And I always add a drop or two of thinner to the bottle when I fill it, as the gutta tends to thicken over time. You'll need only a few drops, though; if it is overly diluted, the gutta will spread out too much on the surface of the silk.

Paints and Dyes for Silk

Silk can be colored with paints or dyes, but both need to be set with either steam or a hot iron to make the colors permanent and washable (see "Steaming and Washing the Silk," page 9). Silk paints are water-based, nontoxic, easy-to-use colors that you dilute with water, and they can be heat-set with a dry iron. They are generally less expensive than silk dyes, and they are a little easier to work with because they mix and clean up easily with water. However, the colors are generally not as bright and rich as dye colors are, which is why I prefer silk dyes.

Silk dyes are professional chemical colors that you thin with a solution of water and rubbing alcohol. They are transparent and blend easily, and they flow beautifully when applied to the silk. The most concentrated types of dyes must be steam-set, but some brands can be set with a liquid fixative or heat-set with an iron. Always read the labels of your dyes for setting instructions. Although I used dyes for the projects in this book, you can substitute silk paints; the colors just won't be quite as brilliant.

Silk Dyes You can purchase premixed colors or mix your own, as I did for the projects in this book. You can mix any color you want from just the three primary colors—red, blue, and yellow—but you might also want to purchase black (to mix with the colors to create darker shades), bright red, royal blue, emerald green, and purple. Different dye manufacturers use different names for the primaries, so check your brand of dyes; I use printer's primaries *magenta, turquoise,* and *lemon yellow.*

IMPORTANT: Steam-set dyes need to be diluted, generally in a ratio of 25% alcohol and 25% water to 50% dye. A good tip is to put equal parts of alcohol and water in a bottle, and then dilute the dyes with 1 part dye to 1 part alcohol/water solution. In the projects in this book, I refer to this as the *standard dilution.*

Painting Safely

Dyes and resists are strong chemicals, so take some precautions when working with them. Always read the directions before using any product, especially the oil-based gutta resists. I use liquid dyes, but if you work with powdered dyes, wear a respiratory mask to keep from breathing in any airborne particles. Also, any kitchen products you use in your artist's studio should never again be used in the kitchen, including the steaming pot and basket used to steam-set the dyes. Finally, protect all surfaces you are painting on with plastic or newspapers. Dyes can permanently stain surfaces, including your carpeting!

Working with Silk

Types of Silk

Silk comes in a variety of weights (5mm, 8mm, and higher) and types of weave. For the projects in this book, I used China silk, crepe de Chine, and charmeuse. China silk (also called "Habotai") is the best type for beginning projects. It's economical and has a smooth surface and an even weave, so the colors flow evenly. Crepe de Chine is a slightly heavier silk used for scarves and other articles of clothing. Silk charmeuse is also heavier, with a very soft feel and a beautiful drape. No matter what kind of silk I choose, though, I prefer white over colored silk. I think the colors look richer and more intense when painted on white or off-white silk.

Fabric stores and specialty textile-painting suppliers sell silk either by the yard (or meter), in precut pieces, or as prehemmed scarves. You can buy pieces of silk clothing and paint them as well, but you can color only the parts you can pin to a frame, which can be difficult with garments that have sewn seams. Some silks can be purchased in PFD (prepared for dyeing) form, which means they don't need to be washed before painting. Always test your silk with dyes or paints first to make sure the silk absorbs the colors. If it seems resistant to the color, hand-wash it in warm water with mild soap (see page 9) before painting.

Silks Silks vary in feel and in the way they react to the colors; try a variety to see what effects you can get. Chiffon, georgette, and organza are translucent silks that cause the dye colors to appear light and delicate. Twill, jacquard, and dupioni are textured silks with a subtle pattern on the surface. Shown here are (top) 8mm Habotai, (bottom) 14mm jacquard , 8mm Habotai, 14mm crepe de Chine, 14mm silk charmeuse, 8mm silk georgette, and 8mm silk chiffon.

Cutting the Silk

Most silk is thin and slick, making it difficult to cut in a straight line. The weave is extremely even, though, so you can get very straight edges by tearing the silk. If your piece has a hem or selvages (the finished edges of fabric), make a small cut through the edge with scissors before tearing. Heavier-textured silks can be difficult to tear. If the silk won't tear easily and seems to pucker, use a straightedge to hold the silk in place, and cut it carefully with scissors instead.

Mounting the Silk

You must always stretch the silk on a frame before painting. Stretching makes the silk taut so the colors won't puddle, and the frame holds the silk away from your work surface. This keeps your surface clean and makes it easier to control the colors and resists you apply to the silk. How you mount the silk will depend on your frame, as shown below (see also page 47).

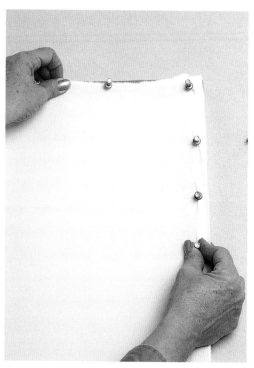

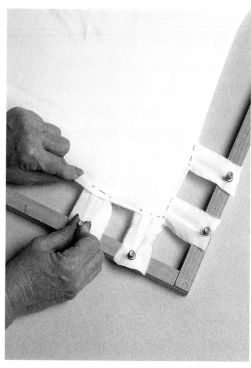

Stretcher Bars Wooden stretcher bars or frames are available in a range of sizes. The frame should be about 2" larger than your silk (for example, use a 22" x 24" frame for a 20" x 22" piece of silk). To mount silk on stretcher bars, first pin the silk to the frame in the center of each side with standard pushpins. Then continue pinning from the center out to the corners, spacing the pins about 2" apart. The goal is to stretch the silk evenly on all sides and to make it very taut. If your frame is too short on one or two sides, follow the procedure for extending the silk, shown at right.

Extending the Silk If the silk piece you have is shorter than your frame, you'll need to add 1"-wide strips of silk that bridge the distance from the frame to the edge of your silk piece. If you don't mind taking the extra steps to pin on extensions, you can save the expense (and storage space!) of investing in a large number of frames of different sizes. Use dressmaker's pins to secure the extensions to your silk piece, attaching an extension about every 3". Then use standard pushpins to attach the extensions to the frame, keeping the silk taut and even (the pins will be about 2" apart).

Steaming and Washing the Silk

I can't stress enough the importance of setting your silk colors properly, especially for clothing that will be exposed to sunlight and washed repeatedly. Steam-setting the silk brightens the colors and melds them into the fabric, making them colorfast and more fade-resistant (see pages 26–29 for details). Some brands of dyes require heat-setting with an iron instead of steam-setting. Follow the directions on the labels, but be careful not to scorch the silk.

Hand-washing silk is not only safe, it also revitalizes the fabric. After setting, hand-wash the silk in warm soapy water, and rinse it under cool running water. Gently squeeze the silk and roll it in a towel to blot it dry. Then place a thin cloth on top of the silk, and press it with a dry iron on a silk setting for 2 to 3 minutes (see page 44). If your silk piece contains oil-based guttas that aren't design elements, dry-clean the piece once to remove the resists; after that, the silk can be hand-washed. (Don't dry-clean guttas that you want to stay in permanently.)

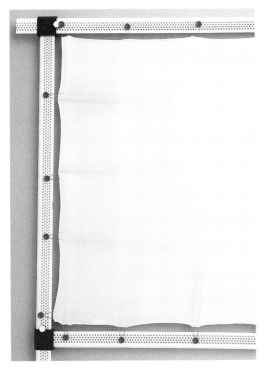

Adjustable Frame An adjustable frame is best if you are going to wet your silk often (wetting the silk before adding colors, or painting wet colors into wet colors), which will make the silk sag. You can adjust the frame repeatedly to take up the slack. Adjustable frames use hooks for attaching the silk, which also makes them a good choice for scarves with rolled edges; the hooks easily attach to the rolled edge so you don't create holes in the scarf itself. First attach the hooks to the frame, and then attach the other end of the hooks through the hem of the silk.

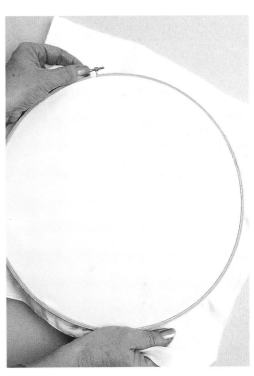

Hoops Embroidery hoops are lightweight and very easy to use—they don't require pinning, and you can pull the silk as often as you need to keep it taut while you paint. Hoops don't come in very large sizes, though, so you'll probably need stretcher bars for large pieces. To use an embroidery hoop, tear the silk slightly larger than the hoop (about 15" square for a 12" hoop, for example). Stretch the silk over the lower hoop while securing the upper hoop on top, and tighten the screw. Pull on the edges as needed to smooth out any puckers.

Learning to Use Silk Dyes: Making a Color Wheel

This color wheel exercise is an excellent introduction to the wonderful art of silk painting. You'll learn to draw on the silk with a washable pencil, outline with gutta resist, create special effects with salt and alcohol, and mix colors. You'll also see why layering and blending with dyes is so important: Because they are transparent, each color changes the others it mixes with or overlaps, creating a new hue. By following my simple steps, you will see how to create 12 vibrant colors from only 3 primaries—and you'll have a beautiful finished silk piece that showcases them all!

Color and Texture Sampler Making a color wheel is a great lesson in mixing color. If you are a beginner, this project will take you through the complete process of dyeing silk and using resists.

What you'll need:

- 15" square 8mm crepe de Chine silk
- 12" embroidery hoop
- paints or your brand of dye's three primaries (red, blue, yellow) in the standard dilution (p. 6)
- clear gutta resist in an applicator with a medium tip
- washable pencil
- cotton swabs
- 10" plastic plate and 6" plastic bowl
- 12 small plastic cups
- sea salt and rubbing alcohol
- small watercolor brush (optional)

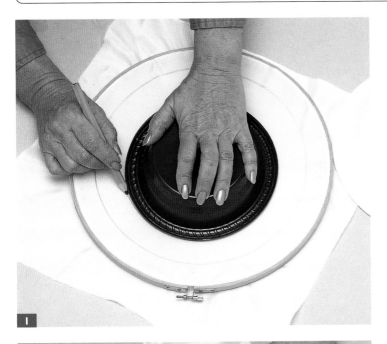

Step One Tear or cut a square piece of silk a few inches larger than the diameter of your hoop. Stretch the silk tightly in the hoop. With a washable fabric pencil, trace around the plastic plate to make a large circle about 1" inside the edge of the hoop frame. Then trace around the bowl to make a smaller circle inside the first circle.

Step Two Divide the area between the two circles into 12 equal parts by first dividing it in half, then dividing it in quarters, and then dividing each quarter into thirds. In the interior of the circle, draw a simple design that consists of at least 6 enclosed shapes, as shown. You can trace an existing design (the silk is transparent enough to see a black line drawing placed beneath it) or draw one freehand, but keep it simple. You can always add more details later.

11

Step Three Fill the applicator bottle with clear gutta resist (see page 5), and use it to trace over the pencil lines, squeezing the bottle gently to get a line of the desired thickness. To learn how much pressure you need to apply, you may want to practice this step on paper before trying it for the first time on silk. Every few minutes, wipe the tip with a paper towel to clean off the built-up gutta. You can also use a straight pin to both clean the tip and keep it sealed when not in use.

Step Four Arrange the 12 cups around the plastic plate. Pour the 3 primary colors (red, yellow, and blue) into 3 cups, keeping 3 empty cups between each color. Dip a cotton swab into one primary, and apply it to one of the sections in the circle. Start from the center, and fill in the space with even, circular strokes. Repeat for each of the 2 remaining colors, leaving three blank sections between each primary.

Step Five Mix the secondary colors (orange, green, and purple) by pouring equal parts of the 2 primary dye colors into the cup between them (pour red and yellow together to make orange, blue and yellow to make green, blue and red to make purple). Make sure you reserve a little of the primary color in the first cups so that you will have enough to mix the tertiary colors. (Refer to the diagram on page 15 if you have any questions about color placement.)

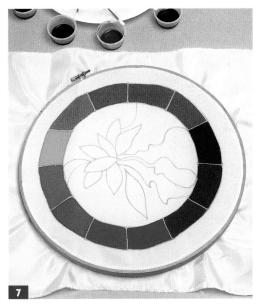

Step Six Apply each secondary color to its appropriate place on the color wheel—in the middle space between the 2 primaries it comprises. Next mix the tertiary colors (yellow-orange, red-orange, yellow-green, blue-green, red-purple, and blue-purple) by pouring equal parts of each primary and each secondary into the cup between them.

Step Seven Using a different cotton swab for each color, finish painting each tertiary color on the wheel until you have all the sections filled. Now you have created all 12 colors for your color wheel in "rainbow" order—warm colors (red, orange, yellow) on one side, and cool colors (green, blue, purple) on the other.

Step Eight Now paint in the center design using any of the colors you have mixed. You may want to use a small watercolor brush instead of a swab, so you can paint the corners more easily. Have a container of clean water ready for rinsing your brush between colors; then use paper towel to blot excess dye off the brush. (If you oversaturate the silk, it will sag.) Use the plastic plate as a palette for mixing new shades.

Step Nine As you fill in the design, get a "feel" for the way your paints or dyes react, and start experimenting with different techniques. Try wetting the shape with water first, and then blend the colors in for a pastel effect; or blend 2 or more colors into one another when they are wet.

Step Ten Next practice creating patterns with salt. Apply a strong saturation of color on a space, and then sprinkle sea salt on the surface while the dye is wet. The salt pulls the color in, creating dark spots in the center and light areas around it. When the silk is completely dry, brush off the salt.

Step Eleven Another special effect is to lighten or lift off color with rubbing alcohol. Let a colored area dry, and then dab it with a cotton swab dipped in undiluted alcohol. Some of the color will come off on the swab, leaving a lighter area within a darker background. When you have finished painting the design, set the colors according to the type of dye or paint you used (steam or heat), and then remove the clear gutta by hand-washing (water-based gutta) or dry-cleaning (oil-based). Then you'll have a completed color wheel for future reference and a sample of the effects achieved with salt, alcohol, and color blends.

Color Wheel Diagram

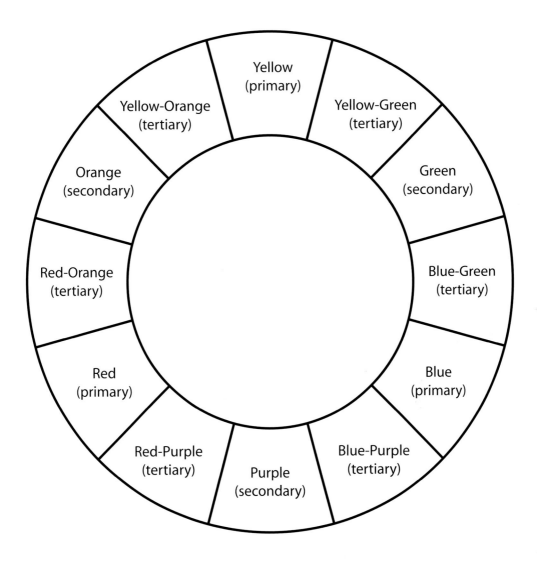

Place the red, blue, and yellow primary colors on the color wheel first (notice that primary blue silk dye looks like turquoise and primary red looks like magenta).
Equal parts of each primary color will produce secondary colors; place each between the appropriate primaries.
Equal parts of one primary and one secondary color will make a tertiary color; place them accordingly.

Variegated Pillows: Texturing with Salt

People have long been attracted to silk painting simply for its sparkling color and strong contrasts of textures. You don't always need to start with a drawn design because the dyes are so beautiful to look at when they're applied freely to the silk, as I did for these pillows. And when the wet dyes or paints react to salt, the effect is immediate, unpredictable, and spectacular— and fascinating to watch! Experiment with different colors and sizes of salt granules to see the effects you can achieve. Then paint a wall hanging or scarf, or try your hand at sewing a pair of colorful accessories for your home!

Free-flowing Design This project requires only two colors and a simple application of salt; it can be done very quickly, but the results are dramatic, and no two pieces will look exactly alike. I've indicated which colors I used for my pillows, but you can choose any colors that fit with your décor.

What you'll need:

- 20" square 14mm crepe de Chine silk (per pillow)
- 22" square frame or wooden stretcher bars (2" larger than the silk square)
- pushpins or tacks

- emerald green and wine red paints or dyes diluted 75% dye to 25% alcohol-and-water solution
- 3" foam brush
- coarse sea salt

Step One Pin the silk to the frame around the outside edges, stretching the silk as tightly as you can (see page 8). Keep in mind that when the silk gets wet it stretches a bit, and you don't want it to touch your work surface. Using the foam brush, apply the wine red dye in broad, horizontal bands as shown.

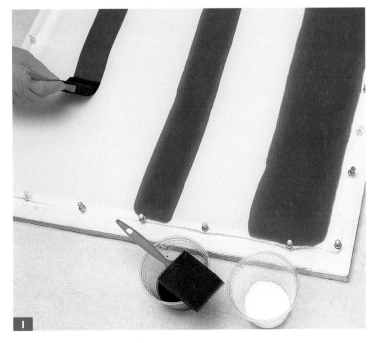

Step Two Working quickly (the dyes dry fairly rapidly), next apply the emerald green in between the red bands, again using broad strokes. Slightly overlap the red and green where they meet, so the colors run together a bit. Notice that the dye solution is stronger than usual (75% dye to 25% dilutant instead of half-and-half) because you want the colors to be quite dark; the salt reaction is more dramatic on dark colors than it is on pastels.

Step Three   As soon as you have finished covering the surface with color, sprinkle a generous amount of sea salt on top of the wet dye. The reaction of the salt to the dye will create a free-form, dappled pattern of lights and darks.

Step Four   Before the silk has a chance to dry, prop up the frame on a slight angle to let the colors run together. Don't angle it so steeply as to cause the salt to slide off, and try not to disturb the salt while the silk is drying.

Step Five   When the silk is completely dry, brush off the salt and remove the silk from the frame. Now the silk can be steamed or heat-set and then washed and ironed (see pages 26–29). If you'd like to make a pillow, add fringe and sew a piece of backing material to the silk. Stuff with batting or a pillow form, and your finished piece is ready for display.

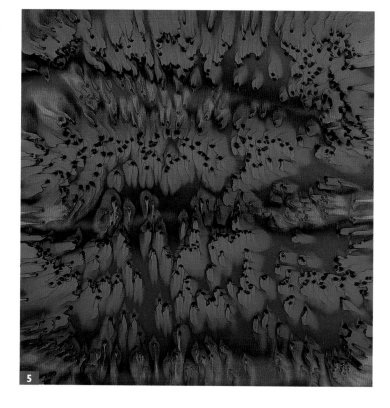

Abstract Bandanna: Alcohol Techniques

For this abstract design, I chose muted earth tones and embellished the edges with an elegant gold gutta border. To create the mottled look, I applied rubbing alcohol to the dyed silk with a cotton swab. Different colors react with the alcohol in different ways, and usually the darker, more subtle colors work the best; browns, greens, and bluish grays are especially attractive when textured with alcohol. Once you've seen how fun and easy this technique is, experiment with other colors and border designs.

Beautiful Bandanna Wearable art can be as complex as a jacket or as simple as this bandanna. The look could be either casual or formal, depending on the border design you use. And, like salt, the alcohol technique is a fast method for creating interesting texture.

What you'll need:

- 22" square white, prehemmed, 8mm China silk scarf
- 24" square wooden stretcher bars or adjustable frame
- any neutral color, such as reddish brown, paints or dyes in the standard dilution
- gold gutta resist in an applicator with a small tip
- pushpins or prongs
- rubbing alcohol (full strength)
- 2" and 3" foam brushes
- two small watercolor brushes
- cotton swabs
- spray bottle

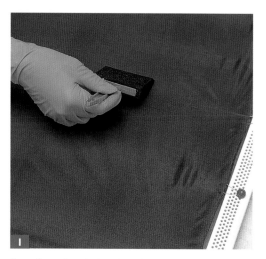

Step One Stretch the silk scarf tightly on the frame, being careful to pin through the hemmed edge only (see page 9). With a 3" foam brush, apply the color over the entire silk surface in broad horizontal strokes, slightly overlapping them for an even coverage. Let the color dry completely.

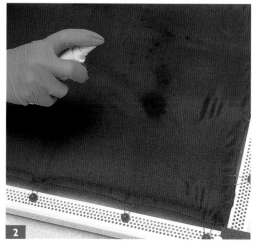

Step Two Now begin creating a variety of patterns with undiluted rubbing alcohol. Try misting first: Spray a mist of rubbing alcohol over sections of the surface, and watch as it starts to dry. Soon you'll see a pattern of large wet and dry spots begin to emerge on the surface.

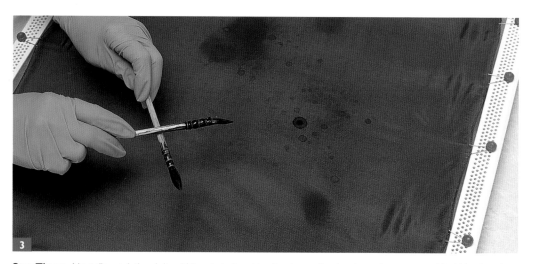

Step Three Next dip a paintbrush in rubbing alcohol, and tap it onto another brush, so that spatters of liquid land on the silk surface. This method produces smaller, more concentrated spots of light areas with dark edges.

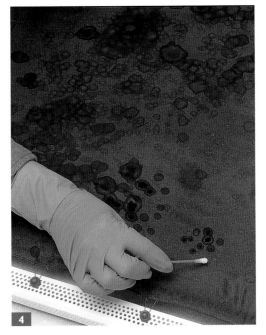

Step Four To create larger "spot circles," dab a cotton swab dipped in undiluted alcohol onto the silk. Touch the silk very lightly, so the circles remain distinct. If you leave the swab on the silk too long, the circles will run together.

Step Five Dip a 2" foam brush into the alcohol, and apply it to the silk in broad strokes. These areas will contrast with the spots and circles, filling out the free-form design. Let the silk dry completely.

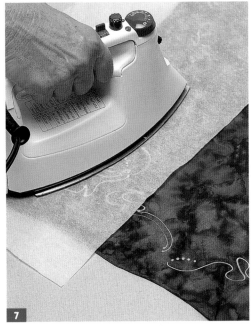

Step Six Add a whimsical pattern of outlines (you can use the template on page 22) with gold gutta applied with a fine-tipped applicator. The design doesn't have to be symmetrical, but the corners should feature special detailing. You could also add another border along the scarf's outer edges.

Step Seven Set the dyes according to their type (see page 9). When the gutta has dried completely, place a piece of fabric or tissue paper over the design. Set a dry iron at medium-high, and iron lightly for about 1 minute to set the gutta. (The gutta can also be set before you set the dyes.)

Bandanna Template

Photocopy the template, enlarging or reducing as needed to fit your silk.

Spring Bouquet:
Clear Gutta Resist Outlines

This lovely floral design with a brilliant blue background is a perfect example of what traditional silk painting is all about. It has bright colors, sharp white outlines around the shapes, and a few special effects created by blending colors and painting into a watered surface. I provide a template for this project, which you can follow or change as you like—or combine parts of the template with other elements to make your own original design. And don't feel constrained to copy the colors exactly; choose those that suit your own taste and décor.

Striking Whites The striking white outlines in this floral painting are produced by using clear gutta resist to reserve the white of the silk. Wall pieces in silk look handsome with no glass over them, but you can frame yours as a watercolor painting using mats and glass if you want to protect it from dust.

What you'll need:

- 22" square 14mm crepe de Chine silk
- 24" square frame or wooden stretcher bars
- pushpins or prongs
- royal blue, pink, primary yellow, primary blue, and black paints or dyes in the standard dilution
- clear gutta in an applicator with a medium tip
- clean water
- watercolor brushes (#2 and #4 for flowers, and #6 or a 1" foam brush for background)
- white drawing paper
- washable pencil

To steam the silk:

- aluminum or enameled pot with a lid
- vegetable steaming basket (plastic or metal)
- hot plate or stove burner
- two pieces of plain newsprint
- 8" square of aluminum foil
- 12" length of string or a rubber band
- large cotton towel
- stack of newspapers (5 or 6 sections)
- weight to place on top of the lid (a brick or a heavy frying pan)
- clean metal soup can with both ends removed

Step One   Copy the template on pages 30–31. If you'd rather create your own design, draw it in pencil on white paper first, and then trace over the lines with a dark marker. The strong marker ink will show through the transparent silk, so you'll easily be able to trace the pattern onto the surface of your silk. (You may want to tape the paper to a tabletop to keep it in place as you draw.)

Step Two   Tape the silk to the paper, and trace the design onto the silk with a washable pencil. Stretch the silk onto a frame (see pages 8–9), but don't worry about getting pinholes in the fabric. This project will probably be best as a framed piece or a pillow, so the edges will not show. Just make sure you make the silk as taut as you can, as it will stretch a little when the dyes are applied.

Step Three   Trace over the lines with clear gutta. The silk in this project is a little heavier than the silk used in the color wheel, so your gutta lines can be slightly thicker. Make sure to enclose all the shapes so that the dyes won't bleed into the wrong area. When you have completed the outline, hold the frame to the light to see if you have missed any spots. If you discover a gap, fill it in with more clear gutta resist. Let the gutta dry.

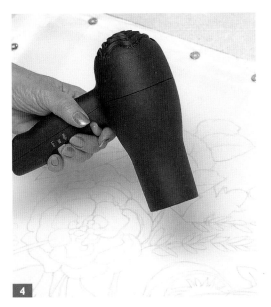

Step Four The gutta must be completely dry before you apply color. Gutta will dry naturally in about one-half hour, but if you want it to dry more quickly, set a hair dryer on high heat, and hold it about 6" away from the surface of the silk. You can tell that the gutta is dry when it has no more shine or is no longer tacky to the touch.

Step Five Begin painting the flowers by first wetting the area inside each petal with water; then carefully apply a little color from one side of the petal to the other, blending as you go. Try not to apply so much water or color that it runs over the lines. If you add too much of either by mistake, blot off the excess with a dry cotton swab.

Step Six To get the graduated light-to-dark effect, wet the silk, and apply a pastel (diluted) color inside the petal shape. While the color is still slightly damp, add a darker shade of the same color along the edge, letting the two shades blend together. Repeat with an even darker shade if desired. The gradations of color will give the flowers dimension.

Step Seven When all the floral details are painted, use a #6 paintbrush or a 1" foam brush to quickly apply the background color to all the open spaces. Begin with the areas between the flowers, and finish with the outside edges.

Step Eight When the color is completely dry, remove the silk from the frame. You can either remove the gutta now (see Step Thirteen) or wait until after you have set the colors.

Step Nine To steam-set the colors, place the silk on top of two sheets of plain newsprint, and roll them together to form a cylinder. (Instead of newsprint, you can use muslin or cotton sheets, which can accommodate very large pieces.)

26

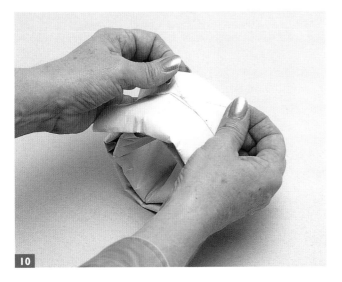

Step Ten Coil the rolled newsprint and silk into a spiral, and secure it with a rubber band or piece of string. Cover the bundle with a square of aluminum foil, but don't enclose it completely (leave the bottom open). The foil will protect the bundle from getting too wet from falling condensation during steaming, but you want the steam to penetrate the bundle to set the dyes properly.

Step Eleven Fill the pot with about 3" of water, and place the hollowed soup can on the bottom of the pot. (The water should not cover the whole can; the steaming basket needs to be elevated above the level of the water.) Set the steaming basket on the can, and place the bundle in the basket. If the bundle fits easily inside the steaming basket, pull the sides of the basket up around the bundle. If the bundle is too large, you can leave the sides lowered, as shown here.

Step Twelve Cover the pot, first with a folded towel and then with sections of newspaper. The towel and paper will absorb excess condensation that forms on the lid during steaming. Place the lid on top of the newspaper. If the lid does not seem secure, weight it with a brick or heavy frying pan. Heat the water to boiling, and let it simmer for 1 hour. Don't leave the pot untended; you don't want the water to boil away before the piece has finished steaming. If the water gets too low before the hour is up, add more boiling water (the water you add must be as hot as the water in the pot, or it will stop simmering, and your silk won't be set when the hour is up).

Step Thirteen When the hour has elapsed, remove the bundle from the heat, and carefully unroll it. The silk should be set properly. If you haven't done so yet, remove the clear gutta by either dry-cleaning the piece (to remove oil-based gutta) or washing it in warm water (to remove water-based gutta). I highly recommend washing the silk again after steaming (see steps 14–18) to remove excess dye or leftover dry-cleaning odors and to smooth out the steamed fabric.

Step Fourteen First run cold water through the silk to remove any excess dye. When the water runs clear, change the water temperature to warm, and plug the drain.

Step Fifteen Add a little mild soap to the warm water, and wash the silk gently but thoroughly. Rinse it under cool running water. To soften it, go on to optional Step Sixteen.

28

Step Sixteen (optional)   Make a rinse bath with a few drops of fabric softener. Remove it from the water, and squeeze gently to remove excess moisture. Then roll the silk in a towel to blot it dry.

Step Seventeen   If you choose not to soften the silk, wait until the silk rinses clear, and then squeeze it gently to remove excess water. Then roll it in a large towel to blot out the rest of the moisture.

Step Eighteen   Set the iron on the silk setting (dry, not steam), and press the silk gently for 2 to 3 minutes. The results should be a bright, soft silk painting with permanently set colors. Your creation can then be framed or sewn as desired.

Spring Bouquet Template

Photocopy both halves of the template, enlarging or reducing as needed to fit your silk. Then overlap the two halves, lining up the registration marks (+) to make a complete template.

Border View: Landscape with Black Gutta Silhouette

This sunset scene is an excellent subject for exploring color gradation techniques. By painting washes of color and applying them in layers from light to dark, you can create dramatic skies, mountains, and other landscape elements. And drawing the silhouette of the tree with black gutta resist (much as you would with a black ink pen) creates a strong contrast against the golds, oranges, and browns of the background. I was inspired to create this landscape one day when I saw the sun set over the California mountains while driving west from Arizona.

Dramatic Sunset This long, narrow piece makes an interesting and striking banner. I sewed under the edges to make a casing at the top and inserted a decorative wrought-iron rod to complement this southwestern design.

What you'll need:

- 15" x 45" 14mm silk charmeuse
- 17" x 47" frame or wooden stretcher bars
- pushpins or prongs
- primary yellow, primary red, primary blue, olive green, forest green, and black paints or dyes in the standard dilution

- clear water-based gutta with applicator
- black gutta with applicator and 2 metal tips (1 fine, 1 medium)
- rubbing alcohol and water for diluting the dyes
- 1" and 3" foam brushes
- #6 flat watercolor brush

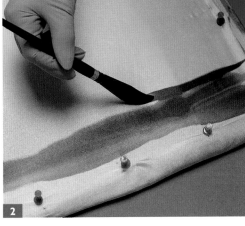

Step One Pin the silk to the frame (see page 8). Mix 5 parts yellow and 1 part red dye to create light gold. Apply this color to the entire surface using a 3" foam brush. Make long horizontal strokes, overlapping them slightly, as you work from the top of the stretched silk to the bottom. Let the color dry completely before going on.

Step Two Mix 3 purple-gray colors. (I used 1 part primary blue to 3 parts primary red; 2 parts blue to 1 part red and 1 part black; and 3 parts blue to 1 part red and 1 part black.) Across the top section, paint about 6 overlapping strokes of the lightest color for clouds. (Don't be alarmed: The colors will look brown when wet.)

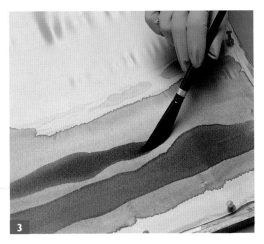

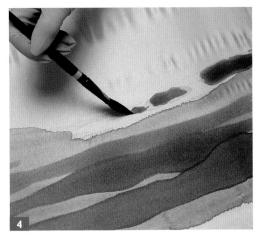

Step Three While the colors are still slightly damp, overlap a few more strokes of the other grays, working from light to dark. Because you are painting into slightly wet colors, the dye will "pool" a bit along the outside, making dark edges. The darkening and slight bleeding on the edges creates a cloudlike effect.

Step Four At the bottom edge of your cloudy sky, add an uneven line made up of a series of dashes in dark purple-gray using a drybrush technique: Wet the brush in dye, and brush it a few times on a paper towel to dry it a bit. With a dryer brush, the colors won't spread very much, so the lowest clouds will stay looking scattered.

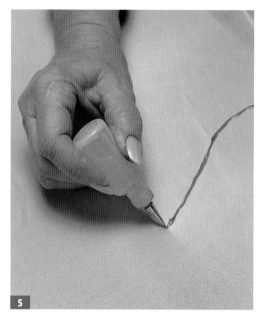

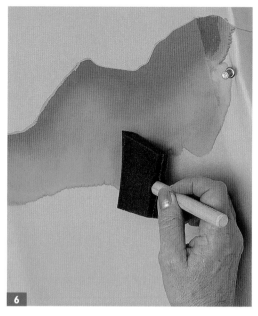

Step Five Now draw a line to represent the farthest mountaintop. (Refer to the final piece on page 35 as needed.) Using clear gutta in an applicator with a medium tip, draw an uneven line across the silk, about a third of the way down. Let the gutta dry completely. Then mix a strong orange color by adding a little yellow to the red.

Step Six Using a 2" foam brush, apply the orange below the gutta line. Bring the color down about two-thirds the surface of the entire silk, leaving some of the gold background at the lower edge. Make a graduated wash by adding a little more water and alcohol solution to each overlapping stroke, so the color fades toward the bottom.

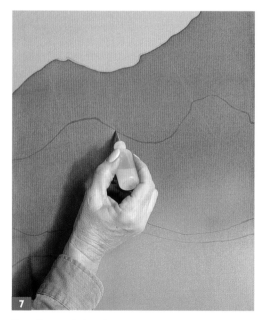

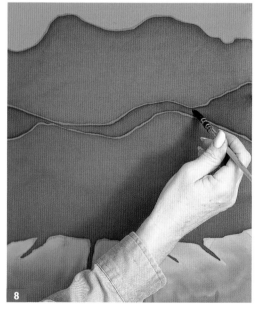

Step Seven When the orange mountain is completely dry, draw another clear-gutta mountaintop line about 2–3" below the first one. Make sure the second line does not repeat the curves of the first one; make it dip in different places so it looks like a separate mountain range. Draw two more gutta lines below that to represent a canyon.

Step Eight Create a rich brown by mixing all three primaries together and adding a little black. With a 1" foam brush, apply this color over the large areas below the gutta mountaintops. Paint a darker shade of brown (add a little more black) in the narrower areas between gutta lines and at the lower portion to show fissures in the rocks.

Step Nine When the mountains and canyons have been painted to your satisfaction, plan the way you want the tree to look. You may want to sketch it with washable pencil first, instead of drawing directly with the gutta. (Remember that you'll need to wash the piece to remove the pencil.) Using black gutta and a fine-tipped applicator, draw bold lines.

Step Ten With a #6 watercolor brush, apply strokes of both greens to the lower part of the silk to represent grasses. Use a dry brush, so the strokes don't blur together, and stroke from the root to the top of the stem. Add as much detail as you like to this section. You might even use clear gutta to outline rocks, fence posts, or small animals.

Step Eleven Let the colors and the gutta dry completely before removing the silk from the stretcher bars. Iron-set the black gutta (see page 21), and steam- or heat-set the colors. Hand-wash the silk to remove the clear gutta, and your project is ready to transform into a beautiful banner or a framed piece of art.

35

Hummingbird and Fuchsias:
Gold Resist over Pastel Colors

The translucent colors and delicate qualities of watercolor paintings are also easily replicated in silk painting. For this project, I borrowed some of the soft blending techniques from that medium and combined them with a simple gold gutta outline. The result is a fanciful design with stylized forms and jewel-like colors that are enhanced by the luster of silk.

Hummingbird Fantasy   For this piece, I again used gutta as a design element, rather than as a resist. I painted the background first, and then I drew the outlines of the the bird and flowers with gold gutta. The stronger colors in the fuchsias and hummingbird make them stand out against the blended pastel background.

What you'll need:

- 22" square 14mm crepe de Chine silk
- 24" square frame or wooden stretcher bars
- pushpins or prongs
- gold gutta resist in an applicator with a fine tip
- primary yellow, primary red, primary blue, and black paints or dyes
- rubbing alcohol and water for diluting dyes
- 1" foam brush and #6 watercolor brush

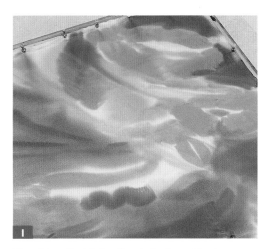

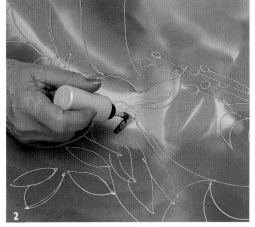

Step One   Stretch the silk onto the frame. To mix very pastel versions of red and blue dyes, put equal parts alcohol and water in a small mixing cup, and then add only a few drops of dye. Mix a few variations of both colors, ranging from very light to medium. Apply swirls of color to the dry silk with a foam brush, blending the colors together slightly but leaving a small amount of the white silk unpainted. Let the colors dry completely.

Step Two   Next create a fanciful line drawing of the fuchsias and hummingbird in gold gutta resist. If you are more comfortable following guidelines, sketch the design onto the silk in washable pencil first, using the templates on page 39. Add some accent lines that follow the swirls of the background colors (see the view of the final piece on page 36 for reference). Then let the gutta air-dry completely, or use a hair dryer to speed up the process (see page 25).

Designing for Fashion

This fashion illustration shows a possible application for a silk painting: appliquéd onto the back of a jacket. Just be sure to choose a jacket (or sew one from scratch) made of fabric that has the same weight as the silk and is similar in color. Appliquéing is also an alternative to painting directly on silk garments that have sleeves and seams; those pieces are difficult to stretch and pin onto a frame.

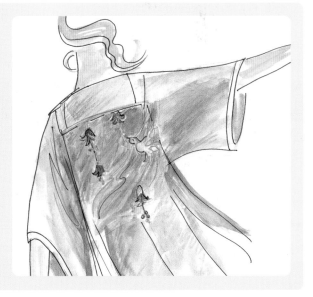

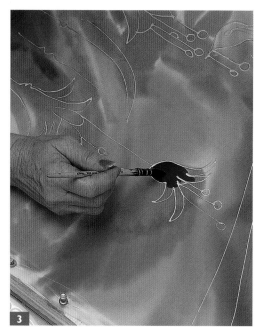

Step Three Mix some stronger concentrations of colors, and begin to fill the areas inside the gold lines for the bird, flowers, and leaves. (Don't fill in the spaces between the accent lines!) I chose shades of red and purple for the fuchsias, and I painted the hummingbird light gray, leaving unpainted white areas for highlights.

Step Four Next add tints of yellow, green, and red in the background. The depth of color is up to you, but I suggest adding a few variations of green using a mixture of blue and yellow. Leave one or two areas lighter than the rest, and darken some spots with rich colors; the light and dark contrasts mimic the effect of sunlight in a garden.

Step Five When the colors are completely dry, remove the silk from the stretcher bars and set as usual. Set the gutta by placing a piece of tissue over the lines, and press with a dry iron at a medium-high setting for about 1 minute.

Step Six Once the gutta is set, hand-wash and let it dry. Then frame your artwork, or turn it into an accessory pillow. You could also incorporate this design into wearable art as the focal point of a jacket (see the box on page 37).

Hummingbird Templates

Photocopy each template, enlarging or reducing as needed to fit your silk.

Classical Koi:
Gutta-Outlined Asian Design

I have been studying Chinese brush painting for some time, and I love the effect of bold brushstrokes on rice paper. I was very pleased with the results I achieved by combining the traditional Chinese painting style with the rich dye colors on silk. For this project, I painted the delicate markings on the backs of the koi using a wet-on-wet technique, and I created streaks of mottled blues and greens with salt and alcohol to represent flowing water.

Colorful Koi This simple yet elegant painting features striking contrasts between the rich blue water and the pale silver koi. And painting wet-on-wet adds to the illusion that the fish are swimming under water.

What you'll need:

- 18" × 26" 14mm crepe de Chine silk
- 20" × 28" frame or wooden stretcher bars
- pushpins or prongs
- bright red, primary yellow, primary blue, royal blue, and black paints or dyes in the standard dilution
- black gutta resist in an applicator with a medium tip
- washable pencil
- #6 watercolor brush
- 1" foam brush

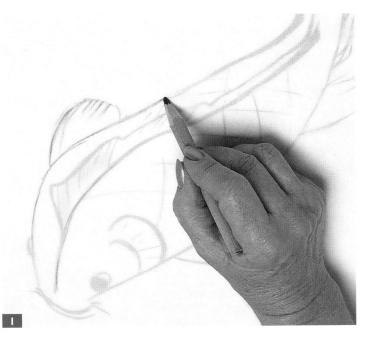

Step One Photocopy the template on page 43, or draw a pattern for the koi on white paper, and trace over lines with black marker so you can see them through the silk. Place the silk over the pattern, and secure it to your work surface with masking tape. Trace the design onto the silk using a washable pencil. Then pin the silk to the frame or stretcher bars, keeping the silk evenly taut.

Step Two Outline the koi with black gutta, using an applicator with a medium tip. Let the gutta air-dry completely, or accelerate the process with a hair dryer, held at least 6" from the silk.

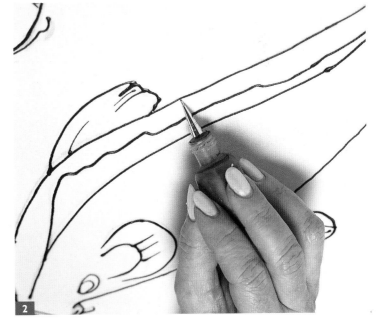

41

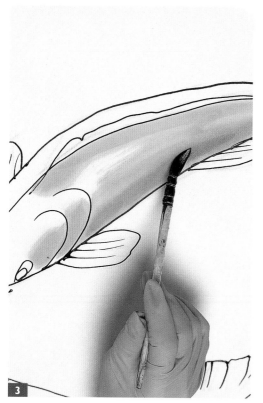

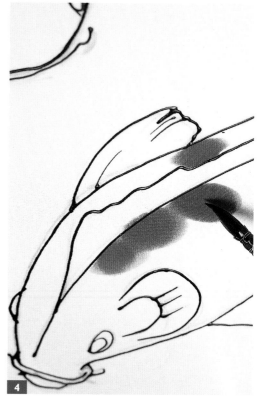

Step Three   Completely cover the surface of each fish with water. Dilute the black to create a soft, light gray, and apply this color inside the fish with a #6 watercolor brush. Leave the head and side unpainted as shown, but be sure to paint the fins and tail gray as well.

Step Four   While the gray is still slightly damp, load your brush with full-strength bright red, and lay the color in dabs along the back of the bottom fish, on either side of the dorsal fin. Make the spots diminish in size as they taper toward the tail. Repeat with full-strength black for the other fish.

Getting Inspired

There is a wealth of inspirational material for designs and painting styles in books, magazines, greeting cards, and art galleries. You may even find designs and patterns on fabrics and upholstery that you'd like to adapt. Take photographs and collect images that appeal to you. Keep them in a box, journal, or expandable file, and you'll always have reference material on hand whenever you want to paint.

Step Five When the red areas on the bottom fish are completely dry, add a few more spots of strong yellow and bright red with a dry brush. Because both the silk and your brush are dry, these spots won't bleed very much; they will be the darkest colors on the fish. Then add strokes of medium gray to the fins and tail as shown.

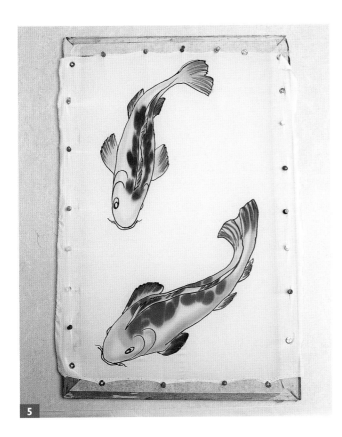

Step Six Paint the background water with mixtures of primary blue and royal blue, applying the color in broad strokes with a 1" foam brush. Before the colors have a chance to dry, sprinkle a little sea salt on the background. Then, when the color is completely dry, brush off the salt. Next streak the surface with a little rubbing alcohol applied with the foam brush, or spatter on spots of alcohol with a watercolor brush tapped against another brush (see page 20).

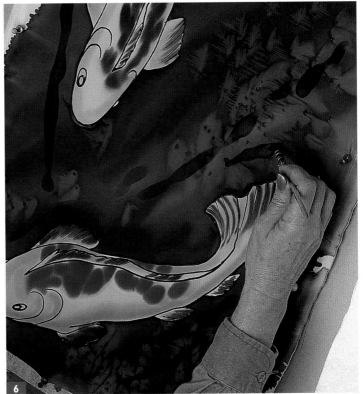

43

Step Seven Now step back and assess your colors and textures. This is the time to add any final accents to the fish or additional streaks in the water with alcohol. Be careful not to overdo it, though; you don't want the background to overpower your subject. When the silk is completely dry, remove it from the stretcher bars and heat- or steam-set as required.

Step Eight This piece does not have to be dry-cleaned because there is no clear gutta to remove, but I do recommend setting the colors and then hand-washing it to remove any excess dye (see pages 28–29). Press the silk through a piece of fabric or tissue paper to set the black gutta and to smooth out any wrinkles. Then your beautiful koi painting is ready to hang or to frame.

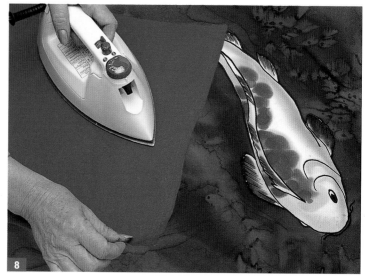

44

Koi Templates

Photocopy each template, enlarging or reducing as needed to fit your silk.

Mystery Dragonflies:
Gutta Resist over Colored Lines

This elegant silk charmeuse scarf was painted with a slightly more advanced technique than I used in previous projects. This time I applied base colors to the silk before drawing with the clear gutta, which gives the illusion that I used colored gutta. I also used variations of several colors in the different elements to create the the illusion of depth. You could simplify your design by painting each element in one color, but why not challenge yourself? Try experimenting with the different effects you can get by layering color on color.

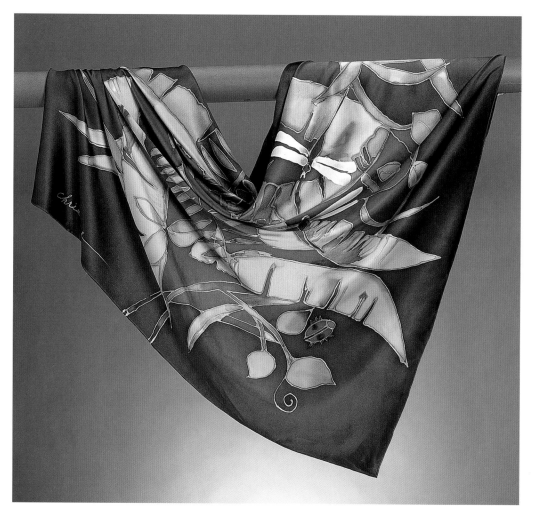

Brilliant Botanical   For this bold, dramatic design, I used both wet-into-wet techniques and an alcohol-water solution to push the colors to the edges of each shape, adding depth and dimension to the composition.

What you'll need:

- 45" square silk charmeuse scarf
- 47" square stretcher bars or stretching frame
- pushpins or prongs
- bright green, dark green, primary red, primary blue, primary yellow, and black paints or dyes
- water and alcohol for diluting the dyes
- clear gutta resist in an applicator with a medium tip
- washable pencil
- #6 watercolor brush
- 1" and 2" foam brushes

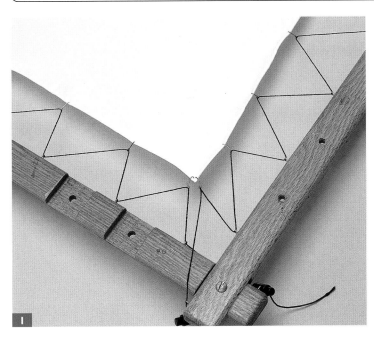

Step One Photocopy the templates on page 51, or draw your design onto white paper, and outline it with black marker. Place the scarf over the pattern, and trace the design onto the silk with a washable pencil. Pin the scarf onto the stretching frame. For the type of frame shown here, first attach the hooks in the corners of the silk to the elastic cord. Attach the middle hook next, and then attach the rest of the hooks in a similar manner, working from the center out to the corners. Pull the cord taut at the toggles. (You can pull the cord through the toggles at any time during painting to tighten the silk.)

Step Two Load a #6 watercolor brush with a strong solution of dye (almost pure color). I used dark green for the leaves, red for the ladybug, and blue for the butterfly. Hold the brush so that it is almost vertical to the silk, and paint over the pencil lines with dye. The dye will spread out about a 1/4" on each side of the pencil line. Don't outline the dragonfly's wings; they will be left unpainted.

Step Three Now trace over the dyed lines with clear gutta, placing the gutta approximately in the center of the dye lines. Later, when you paint your colors inside the lines, the dyes will flow up to the gutta and overlap the dyed lines, making the edges of each shape appear to be in shadow.

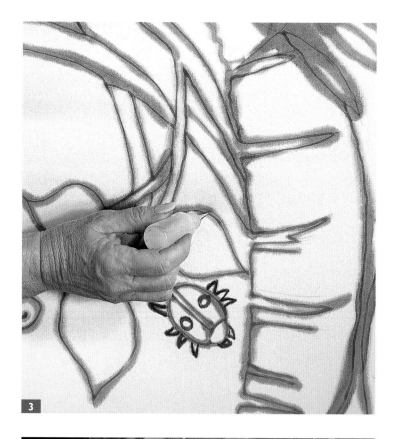

Step Four Begin painting the leaves with various shades of green and yellow, adding a few areas of orange for interest. Let the colors flow together inside the gutta lines, but leave some unpainted white areas for highlights. Paint the ladybug and the flower in shades of red, the butterfly in shades of blue, and the other bug in purples. For the dragonfly bodies, I mixed blue with a little bit of red to make a purple-blue.

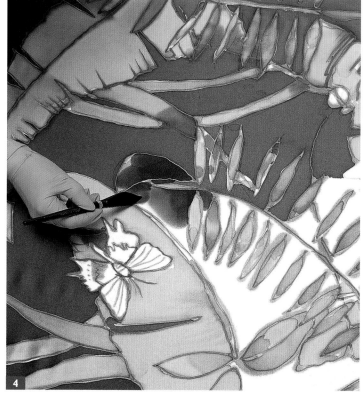

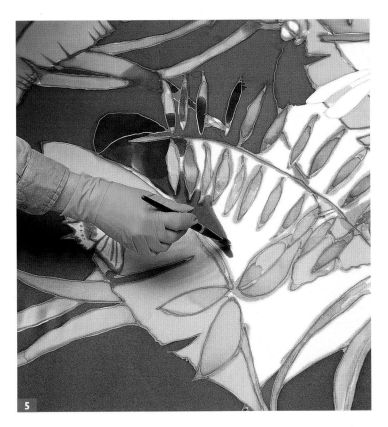

Step Five Fill in the background with an even application of deep color. I used dark green, but you could also use navy blue or black. Any dark color will make the other elements "pop out" from the background.

Step Six After the colors are dry, mix a half-and-half solution of rubbing alcohol and water, and paint this solution over any areas where the colors look spotty. The alcohol solution re-wets the colors and acts as a blending medium, moving the colors around and unifying them. If you find there are areas that need to be darker, you can also add color to the blending solution.

Step Seven When the colors are completely dry, remove the scarf from the stretcher bars and heat- or steam-set the colors. Dry-clean or hand-wash the scarf to remove the gutta resist, and it's ready to wear!

Caring for Your Wearable Silk Pieces

Once you've invested time and energy into painting your silk, you'll want to make sure you care for it properly. Obviously, you shouldn't bleach your silk, but also avoid exposing it to sunlight for extended periods of time. Store silk clothing on padded hangers, and press them with a dry iron if they become wrinkled. Perspiration can stain silk, so hand-wash—never machine wash—your silk pieces often.

Dragonfly Templates

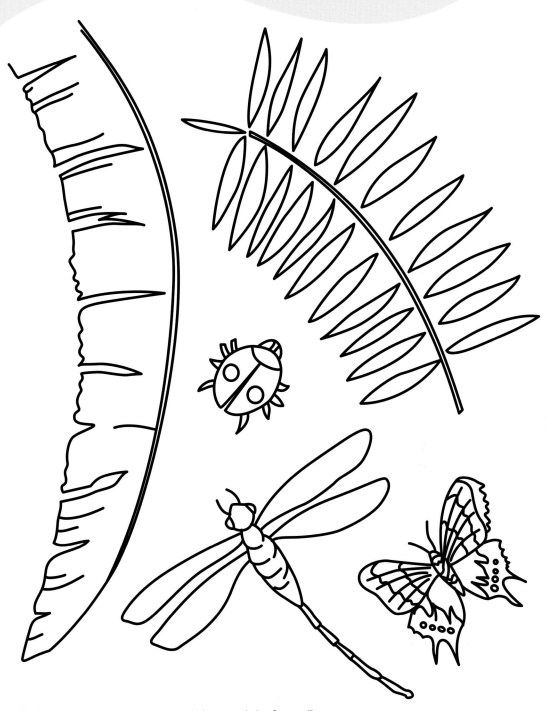

Photocopy each template, enlarging or reducing as needed to fit your silk.

Tropical Explosion:
Wax-Resist Technique

One of the things I like best about silk dyes is the brilliant colors they produce—regardless of the design I choose. This colorful scarf will coordinate with most any outfit and will beautifully set off a plain one. To create the pattern, I used a batik technique; I painted on hot wax as a resist, colored over it with dyes, and then dissolved the wax to remove it. My scarf has a very abstract design, so don't worry about duplicating it exactly; it's the color that counts.

Beautiful Batik   For this colorful piece, I used a hot-wax resist technique instead of gutta resist. The effect is similar, but with wax, you can get a thicker line than you can with gutta.

What you'll need:

- 15" x 60" 8mm prehemmed crepe silk scarf
- 17" x 62" frame or wooden stretcher bars
- pushpins or prongs
- wax tools (see box below)
- rubber gloves
- fuchsia, primary red, primary yellow, primary blue, and royal blue paints and dyes in the standard dilution
- 3" foam brush
- sea salt

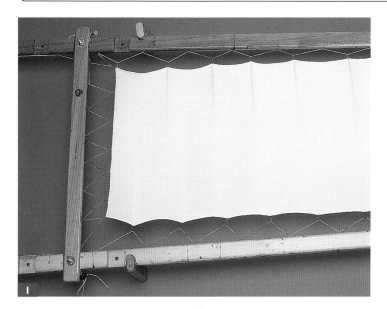

Step One   Stretch the scarf onto the stretcher bars or silk stretching frame (see page 47 for instructions on using this type of frame). Make sure the frame lies flat and is elevated about 6" off the table or floor. The pressure of the brush and weight of the wax will cause the silk to sag somewhat, and you don't want the silk to touch your work surface.

Working with Hot Wax

The batik technique requires that you melt wax, so you'll need a few extra supplies for this project. I recommend using a small electric frying pan—one that will be used exclusively for melting wax—and a combination of 1/2 lb beeswax and 1/2 lb paraffin for the resist. You'll also need to sacrifice a 2" pastry brush with a wooden handle (it will rest against the side of the pan) and a bamboo brush; both will be unusable for anything but wax application after this!

Step Two Create gold by mixing 4 parts primary yellow to 1 part primary red dye. With a 3" foam brush, liberally apply the gold color, diluted according to standard proportions. Make random strokes, and leave some white areas for the second color, fuchsia. These are the base colors that will remain in the design after the wax is removed.

Step Three Before the gold dries, quickly apply fuchsia in between the gold areas. As you add the fuchsia, let the strokes overlap the edges of gold and run together.

Step Four Next sprinkle sea salt over the wet colors. Tip one corner of the frame to make the dyes run diagonally. Let the colors dry completely, and then brush off the salt.

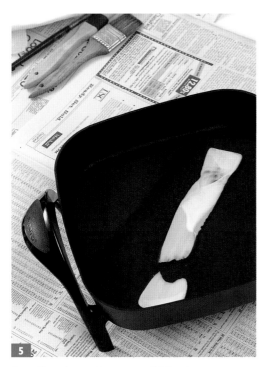

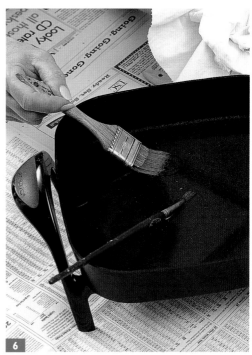

Step Five Set the frying pan to 275°, and melt a mixture of 1/2 lb beeswax and 1/2 lb paraffin wax. Don't stir the wax while it is melting.

Step Six In about 10 minutes, the wax should be completely melted. Set the brushes in the hot wax, and let them rest for 2 minutes to soften the bristles.

Step Seven Carefully paint the wax on the silk with wild floral patterns (see Step Eight), and keep a paper towel in your opposite hand to catch any wax drips. Remember that, when you finish painting and remove the wax, whatever you have covered with wax will remain the color of the dye underneath, even though the color appears to darken at this stage.

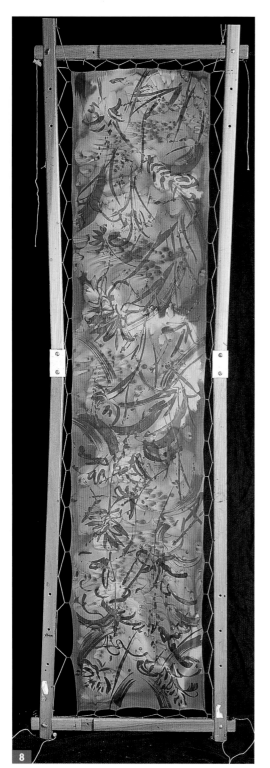

Step Nine Mix primary blue and royal blue to make deep teal, and apply the color with a 3" foam brush. Although the wax will resist the dye, try not to paint directly over the wax; paint around it as much as possible.

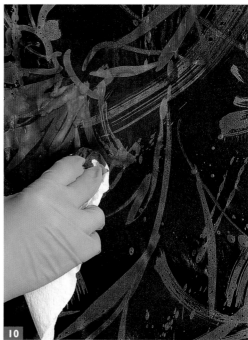

Step Eight Use this full-size view as a guideline for your floral patterns, altering the design as much or as little as you wish. When you are happy with your design, let the wax dry completely before continuing (approximately 2 minutes).

Step Ten If you accidentally brush over the wax with dye, the color will bead up on its surface. Wipe it clean with a paper towel before the dye has a chance to dry. And wear rubber gloves for this step: it can be messy!

Step Eleven   When all the dyes are dry, remove the silk from the frame, and place it between two sheets of plain newsprint paper. Set a dry iron on a medium-high setting, and iron over the paper. The heat will cause the wax to dissolve, and it will be absorbed by the newsprint.

Step Twelve   When you've finished ironing off the wax, the scarf will feel a little stiff, but it will soften when it's dry-cleaned. Steam the piece as usual to set the dyes, and then have the scarf dry-cleaned to remove the last remnants of wax.

Interior Still Life: Painting a Scene

For this interior, I designed a scene that brought back memories of sunny afternoons in a seaside cottage in Laguna Beach, California. I wanted to create a warm room to contrast with a cooler exterior view through the French windows. I included my friend's cat, Lady Tux, because she would enjoy resting on a wicker lounge chair just about anytime during the day. Here I used the standard method of silk painting: sectioning with gutta and layering colors.

Afternoon Interior   For this project, I added a few accent lines to the final painting with permanent marking pen.

What you'll need:

- 24" x 34" 12mm China silk
- 26" x 36" frame or wooden stretcher bars
- pushpins or prongs
- colors of your choice, or primary red, primary yellow, primary blue, and black paints or dyes in the standard dilution
- water and rubbing alcohol for diluting the dyes
- clear gutta in an applicator with a fine tip
- #6 and #2 watercolor brushes
- washable pencil
- black permanent marker

Step One Draw your design on paper, and outline it with a black marker. Place the silk over the pattern, and trace the design onto the silk with a washable pencil. Pin the silk to the frame very tightly, keeping the lines on your design straight and even.

Step Two Outline all the pencil lines with clear gutta, but don't add the details on the interior patterns (on the quilt, the tablecloth, and the curtains). They will come later. Let the gutta dry completely before applying any color.

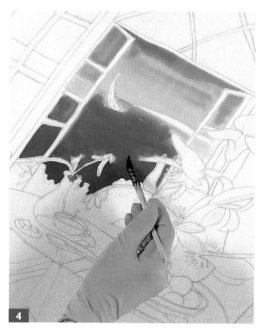

Step Three Mix a variety of colors before you start; I suggest mixing different shades of all 12 colors from the color wheel exercise (see pages 10–14). Then you can paint freely, without stopping to mix each new color. Begin by applying a pale blue graduated wash for the sky: wet the silk with water, and float the light blue into the water, using less color as you move toward the water line. Leave an unpainted area in the middle to resemble white clouds.

Step Four Wet the area for the ocean, and then apply a blue-green wash, making the area near the horizon a little lighter and strengthening the color toward the bottom. This is another graduated wash, but instead of working dark to light the color graduates from light to dark. The two washes add depth to the scene; because the darks are in the foreground and the lighter colors are near the horizon, the sky and water appear to recede into the distance.

Step Five Paint the window frame with light lavender, and add shades of gray or another neutral to create a shadow on the moulding around the window frame. Plain white often looks as if it were left unpainted by mistake, and adding a little gray or neutral gives the effect of a three-dimensional door frame.

60

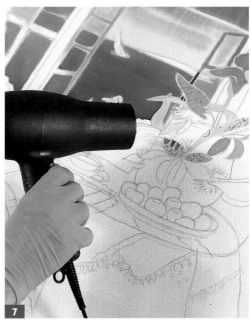

Step Six Begin laying in the colors for the other elements, putting a light coat of dye on each area. You can always go back later and touch up a spot, add a second color over the first, or add a pattern by using gutta over the color. Start with the plant on the table, painting the leaves with shades of green.

Step Seven Next begin adding veins and patterns. Draw the outlines with gutta, and then fill in the shapes with color. You must let the silk dry completely before applying gutta, so you might want to use a hair dryer to speed up the drying process in between colors. Just be sure to hold the dryer at least 6" away from the silk.

Step Eight Keep adding veins, patterns, and details to the leaves by applying gutta and painting in darker greens, always working from light to dark. Then use the same process to paint the fruit and other items on the table, applying gutta and adding different colors. When you've finished with the tabletop, paint in the colors on the potted plant to the left of the cat.

Step Nine Next paint the cat. Start with a very pale gray by diluting black dye for the lightest values—where the fur is white. Add gutta outlines on the areas to be painted light brown (mix the three primaries and dilute the mix), and then apply that color. Outline and paint the black section last.

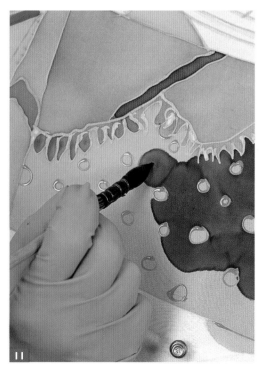

Step Ten Now paint the pillows behind the cat. Draw outlines for fern leaves with gutta, and fill them in with shades of green. I painted the background with a pinkish-gray (diluted black with a little red), and then colored the back pillow with primary blue mixed with just a little yellow.

Step Eleven Next add patterns on the tablecloth and quilt, outlining in gutta and adding layers of color. Remember: Work from light to dark, and let the colors dry between layers. Also keep in mind that each translucent color you add will be altered slightly by the color beneath it.

Step Twelve For the curtains, draw delicate floral designs in gutta. Where the fabric folds, draw only half of the pattern, to give the illusion that it continues around the fold. Here I used purple, green, and yellow for the flowers. For the background, I used a mauve which I created by mixing red with a neutral—gray—to soften the color. To show the shadows in the folds, I applied a little darker gray into the mauve while it was only slightly damp.

Step Thirteen Remove the silk from the frame, and set as usual. Then dry-clean or hand-wash the piece to remove the gutta. To add final details, stretch the silk over a piece of foam core board. Tape the silk to the back of the board, keeping the silk very taut. Then, with a permanent marker, draw in additional details, such as more realistic fur on the cat. Add stronger lines around any element that disappeared when the silk was dry-cleaned. When you're satisfied, remove the silk from the board and it's ready for framing and hanging!

Conclusion

I hope that I have inspired you to try this beautiful art form. If you'd like to learn more, I encourage you to enroll in a class. Classes in silk painting are offered as part of many adult education and recreation programs, and several nationally known artists offer workshops at art centers or retail stores. Check out these opportunities to discover tips and learn new techniques from other professionals, who can offer suggestions on how to make your creations more artistic. Then experiment with different silks, colors, and techniques—nothing can take the place of hands-on experience. And use your imagination! Soon you'll discover your own style, and your creations will be as unique as you are. Most of all, enjoy yourself!

Expand Your Horizons Silk painting is a wonderful form of self-expression and a great outlet for artistic creativity. Don't be afraid to try something new and challenging, and don't be afraid of making mistakes. Remember: What may start as a mistake can turn out to be a "happy accident!"